Cross Stitch

Festive Christmas Stockings

You'll want to hang these exquisite stockings by the chimney with care so St. Nick can fill them with delightful holiday treats!

LEISURE ARTS, INC. • Maumelle, Arkansas

Celestial Angels Stocking

Designed by Barbara Sestok

Christmas cherubs descend through the evening sky to share greetings of peace, joy, and noel to all. Shimmering glass star beads scatter through the midnight clear to create a unique gift for someone special.

Note: Please read all instructions on page 33 before beginning.

Stitch Count= 126w × 204h

Fabric

- One 18" × 21" (45.7cm × 53.3cm) piece of 28-ct. Colonial Blue Lugana® by Zweigart® (stitched over two threads)

Design Size

- 28-ct. = 9" × 14½" (22.9cm × 36.8cm)

Embellishments

- 1 package each of White #00479 and Victorian Gold #02011 glass seed beads by Mill Hill®
- 1 package of Oriental Red #03043 antique glass seed beads by Mill Hill
- 41 #12165 Crystal Bright Small 5-Pointed Star treasures by Mill Hill

FINISHING MATERIALS

- One 14" × 20" piece of coordinating fabric for backing
- Two 14" × 20" pieces of coordinating fabric for lining
- 1½ yards of ¼-wide cording
- Matching sewing thread

GENERAL INSTRUCTIONS

Center the design and begin stitching over two fabric threads. Use two strands of cotton embroidery floss or Kreinik very fine (#4) braid for cross stitches and lazy daisy stitches. Work backstitches and straight stitches with one strand of cotton embroidery floss or Kreinik very fine (#4) braid. Lightly press from the back before attaching beads and treasures with one strand of coordinating cotton embroidery floss. (When representing the stars in the sky, the beads and treasures may be placed at random; the bead placement on the chart is merely a guide.)

FINISHING INSTRUCTIONS

Use a ½" seam allowance for all sewing unless otherwise specified. Center and trim the needlework to within 1" of the stitching. With the wrong side up, use the needlework as a template to cut two pieces from the right side of coordinating fabric. Flip the needlework right side up and use it as a template to cut one piece from the right side of coordinating fabric.

Cut 1½"-wide bias strips of coordinating fabric and piece together to form one 34"-long strip. Fold in half lengthwise with wrong sides together. Insert cording into the fold and sew tightly along the edge of the cording using a zipper foot. Making sure the cording is flush with the edge of the stitching, start at the top left of the needlework and sew the piping around the stocking, keeping the seam close to the cording.

With right sides together, sew the stocking front to the back, sewing tight to the cording but leaving the top open. Trim the side and bottom seam allowances to ¼". Turn the stocking right side out and iron using a pressing cloth.

Sew the lining pieces together in the same manner as the stocking, but use a 1" seam allowance and leave a 4" opening along the bottom of the "foot" for turning. Trim the side and bottom seam allowances to ¼".

Leave the lining wrong side out and insert the stocking into the lining, aligning the top edges. Sew all the way around the top, sewing through all layers. Pull the stocking through the opening in the lining. Slipstitch the opening in the lining. Tuck the lining inside the stocking and press.

Cut a 3" × 6" strip of coordinating fabric for a hanging loop. With right sides together, fold in half lengthwise and press. Sew along the cut edge, turn, and fold in half to form a loop. Attach to the top right inner corner of the stocking with a few hand-stitches.

Chart Layout

A	B
C	D

JOY
NOEL

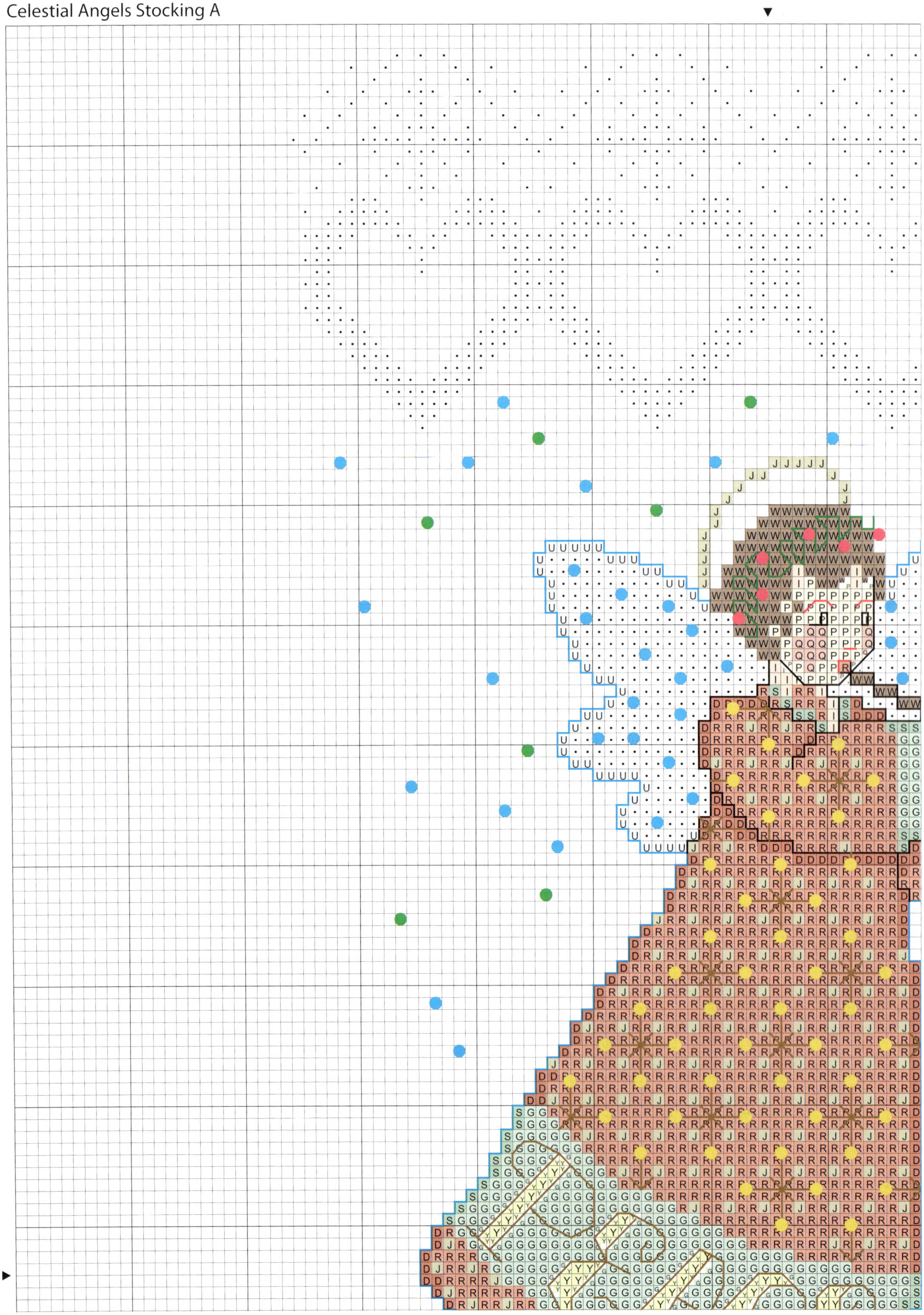

Celestial Angels Stocking B

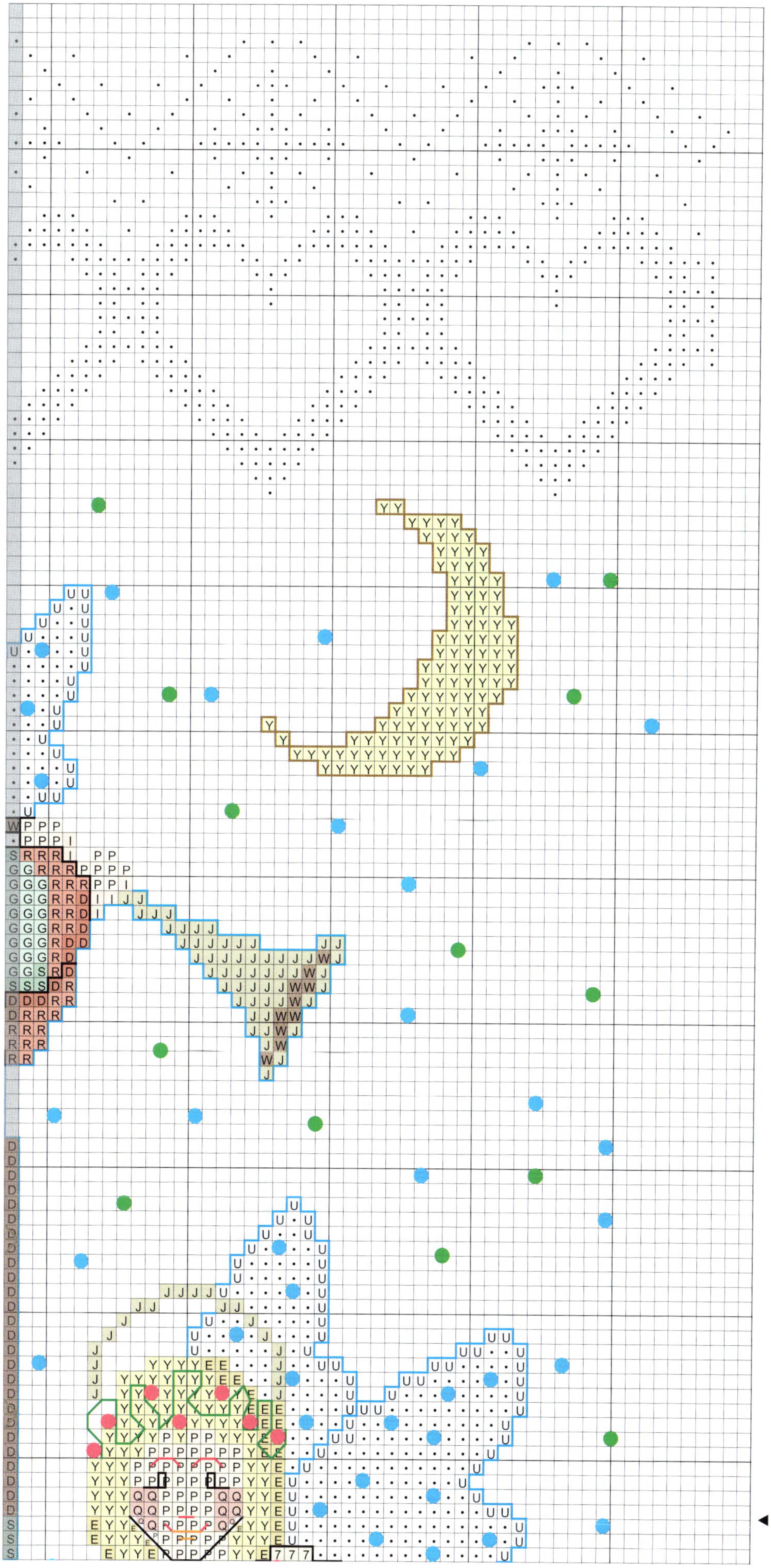

CROSS STITCH

ANCHOR		DMC	COLOR
002	·	White	White
120	U	157	Very Light Cornflower Blue
352	W	300	Very Dark Mahogany
1049	A	301	Medium Mahogany
310	N	434	Light Brown
1045	T	436	Tan
046	D	666	Bright Christmas Red
295	Y	726	Light Topaz
305	E	728	Topaz
300	L	745	Light Pale Yellow
882	I	758	Very Light Terra Cotta
923	S	909	Very Dark Emerald Green
209	G	912	Light Emerald Green
881	P	945	Tawny
036	Q	3326	Light Rose
035	R	3801	Light Christmas Red
386	7	3823	Ultra Pale Yellow

KREINIK BRAID #4		COLOR
002	J	Gold

BACKSTITCH

ANCHOR	DMC	COLOR
352	300	Very Dark Mahogany

KREINIK BRAID #4	COLOR
001	Silver
003	Red
005	Black
008	Green

STRAIGHT STITCH

ANCHOR	DMC	COLOR
035	3801	Light Christmas Red

KREINIK BRAID #4	COLOR
002	Gold

LAZY DAISY

ANCHOR	DMC	COLOR
209	912	Light Emerald Green

BEAD

MILL HILL GLASS SEED	COLOR
00479	White
02011	Victorian Gold

MILL HILL ANTIQUE GLASS SEED	COLOR
03043	Oriental Red

MILL HILL TREASURE	COLOR
12165	Crystal Bright Star

Gray area indicates last row of previous section of design.

Celestial Angels Stocking C

Celestial Angels Stocking D

CROSS STITCH

ANCHOR		DMC	COLOR
002	•	White	White
120	U	157	Very Light Cornflower Blue
352	W	300	Very Dark Mahogany
1049	A	301	Medium Mahogany
310	N	434	Light Brown
1045	T	436	Tan
046	D	666	Bright Christmas Red
295	Y	726	Light Topaz
305	E	728	Topaz
300	L	745	Light Pale Yellow
882	I	758	Very Light Terra Cotta
923	S	909	Very Dark Emerald Green
209	G	912	Light Emerald Green
881	P	945	Tawny
036	Q	3326	Light Rose
035	R	3801	Light Christmas Red
386	7	3823	Ultra Pale Yellow

KREINIK BRAID #4		COLOR
002	J	Gold

BACKSTITCH

ANCHOR	DMC	COLOR
352	300	Very Dark Mahogany

KREINIK BRAID #4	COLOR
001	Silver
003	Red
005	Black
008	Green

STRAIGHT STITCH

ANCHOR	DMC	COLOR
035	3801	Light Christmas Red

KREINIK BRAID #4	COLOR
002	Gold

LAZY DAISY

ANCHOR	DMC	COLOR
209	912	Light Emerald Green

BEAD

MILL HILL GLASS SEED	COLOR
00479	White
02011	Victorian Gold

MILL HILL ANTIQUE GLASS SEED	COLOR
03043	Oriental Red

MILL HILL TREASURE	COLOR
12165	Crystal Bright Star

Gray area indicates last row of previous section of design.

Nordic Santa Stocking

Designed by Barbara Sestok

This gorgeous depiction of St. Nick makes a striking stocking that will be treasured for many years. Personalizing the cuff adds the perfect finishing touch!

Notes: Please read all instructions on page 33 before beginning. Use the alphabet on pages 14-15 to chart and center the desired name on the cuff area.

Stitch Count= 136w × 213h

FABRIC

• One 17" × 23" (43.2cm × 58.4cm) piece of 28-ct. Blue Country French Linen fabric by Wichelt Imports (stitched over two threads)

DESIGN SIZE

• 28-ct. = 9¾" × 15¼" (24.8cm × 38.7cm)

EMBELLISHMENTS

• 1 package each of Old Gold #00557 and Autumn Flame #02034 glass seed beads by Mill Hill®

FINISHING MATERIALS

• 1 yard of coordinating cotton fabric for backing and lining

• Matching sewing thread

GENERAL INSTRUCTIONS

Center the design and begin stitching over two fabric threads. Work all stitches with two strands of cotton embroidery floss. Work each half stitch from the lower left corner to the upper right. Using the alphabet provided, personalize the stocking with the desired name, making sure to center the name on the cuff. Attach beads using one strand of coordinating floss. Place the needlework facedown on a terry cloth towel (to protect the beads) and use a pressing cloth to carefully iron the needlework from the back before finishing.

FINISHING INSTRUCTIONS

Trim the needlework to within 1" of the stitching on all sides. With the wrong side up, use this piece as a template to cut two stocking shapes from the right side of coordinating fabric. Flip the needlework right side up and use it as a template to cut one piece from the right side of the lining fabric. With right sides together, sew the stocking front to the backing piece, sewing tight to the edge of the stitching but leaving the top open. Trim the side and bottom seam allowances to ½". Turn the stocking right side out and iron using a pressing cloth. Sew the lining pieces together in the same manner as the stocking, but use a 1" seam allowance and leave a 4" opening along the bottom of the "foot" for turning. Trim the side and bottom seam allowances to ½". Leave the lining wrong side out and insert the stocking into the lining, aligning the top edges. Pin in place. Sew all the way around the top along the edge of the stitching, sewing through all layers. Pull the stocking through the opening in the lining. Slipstitch the opening in the lining, tuck the lining inside the stocking, and press. Create a small hanging loop by cutting a 1¾" × 5" strip from leftover fabric. Fold in half along the length with right sides together and press. Sew along the cut edge, turn right sides out, and fold in half to form a loop. Attach the hanging loop to the top right corner of the stocking with a few hand-stitches.

Jessica

CROSS STITCH

ANCHOR		DMC	COLOR
387	S	Ecru	Ecru
120	V	157	Very Light Cornflower Blue
009	K	352	Light Coral
1046	F	435	Very Light Brown
1045	R	436	Tan
877	H	502	Blue Green
334	T	606	Bright Orange Red
226	a	702	Kelly Green
256	U	704	Bright Chartreuse
305	Y	728	Topaz
300	>	745	Light Pale Yellow
175	r	794	Light Cornflower Blue
271	3	819	Light Baby Pink
162	t	825	Dark Blue
161	4	826	Medium Blue
360	9	839	Dark Beige Brown
388	E	842	Very Light Beige Brown
333	P	900	Dark Burnt Orange
340	6	919	Red Copper
881	b	945	Tawny
246	A	986	Very Dark Forest Green
244	J	987	Dark Forest Green
242	M	989	Forest Green
1040	W	3023	Light Brown Gray
397	G	3024	Very Light Brown Gray
360	N	3031	Very Dark Mocha Brown
871	<	3041	Medium Antique Violet
869	n	3743	Very Light Antique Violet
120	8	3747	Very Light Blue Violet
336	k	3771	Ultra Very Light Terra Cotta
306	+	3820	Dark Straw
002	O	3865	Winter White

HALF STITCH (symbols appear as full stitches in chart)

ANCHOR		DMC	COLOR
300	B	745	Light Pale Yellow
023	=	818	Baby Pink
006	e	967	Very Light Apricot

FRENCH KNOT

ANCHOR		DMC	COLOR
226	•	702	Kelly Green
256	•	704	Bright Chartreuse
305	•	728	Topaz
360	•	3031	Very Dark Mocha Brown
306	•	3820	Dark Straw

Color key continued on page 11.

BACKSTITCH

ANCHOR	DMC	COLOR
009	352	Light Coral
334	606	Bright Orange Red
256	704	Bright Chartreuse
305	728	Topaz
162	825	Dark Blue
360	839	Dark Beige Brown
379	840	Medium Beige Brown
340	919	Red Copper
246	986	Very Dark Forest Green
360	3031	Very Dark Mocha Brown
306	3820	Dark Straw
002	3865	Winter White

STAR EYELET

ANCHOR	DMC	COLOR
305	728	Topaz

BEAD

MILL HILL GLASS SEED	COLOR
00557	Old Gold
02034	Autumn Flame

Gold area indicates last row of previous section of design.

Nordic Santa Stocking C

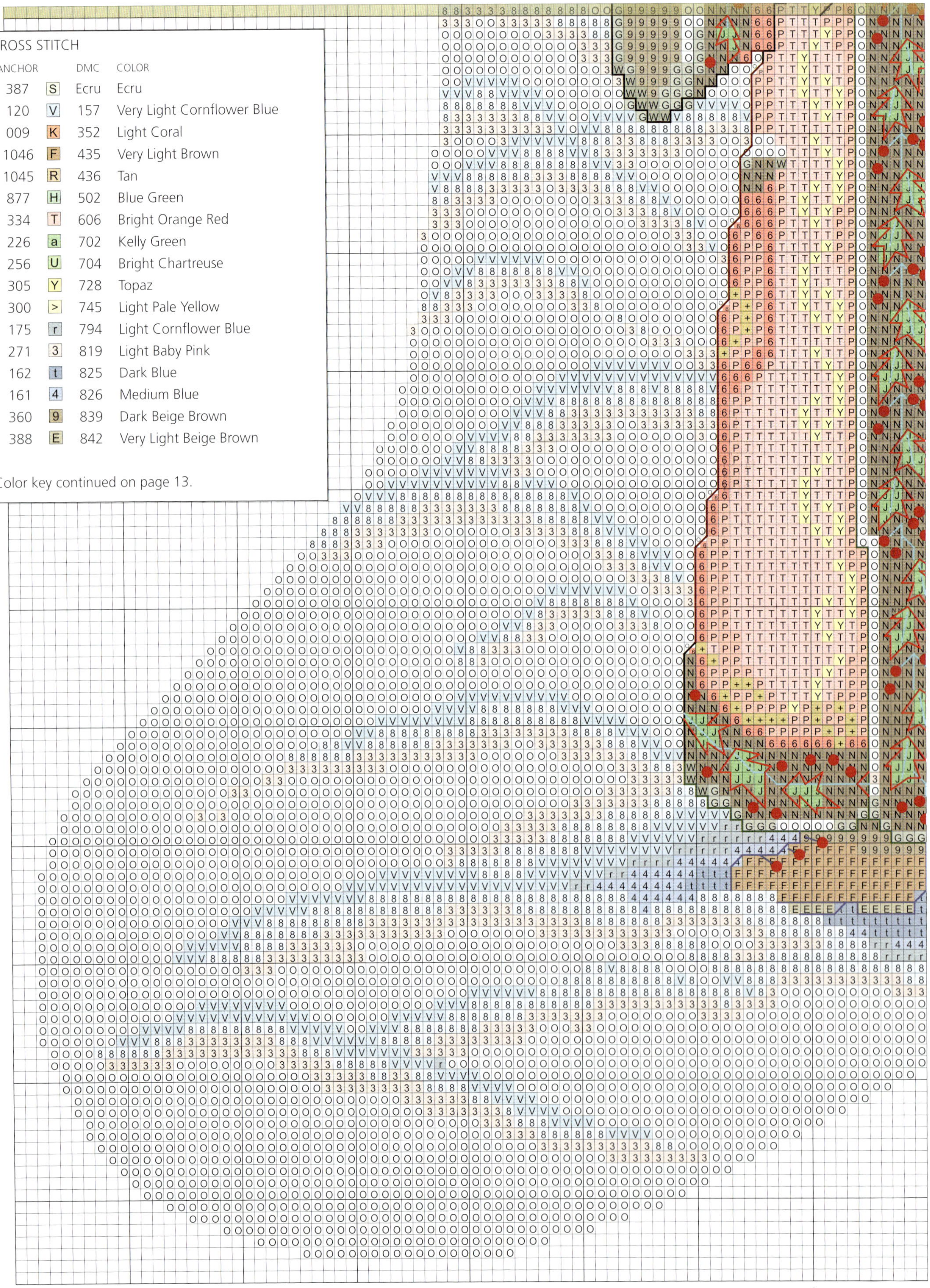

CROSS STITCH

ANCHOR		DMC	COLOR
387	S	Ecru	Ecru
120	V	157	Very Light Cornflower Blue
009	K	352	Light Coral
1046	F	435	Very Light Brown
1045	R	436	Tan
877	H	502	Blue Green
334	T	606	Bright Orange Red
226	a	702	Kelly Green
256	U	704	Bright Chartreuse
305	Y	728	Topaz
300	>	745	Light Pale Yellow
175	r	794	Light Cornflower Blue
271	3	819	Light Baby Pink
162	t	825	Dark Blue
161	4	826	Medium Blue
360	9	839	Dark Beige Brown
388	E	842	Very Light Beige Brown

Color key continued on page 13.

Nordic Santa Stocking D

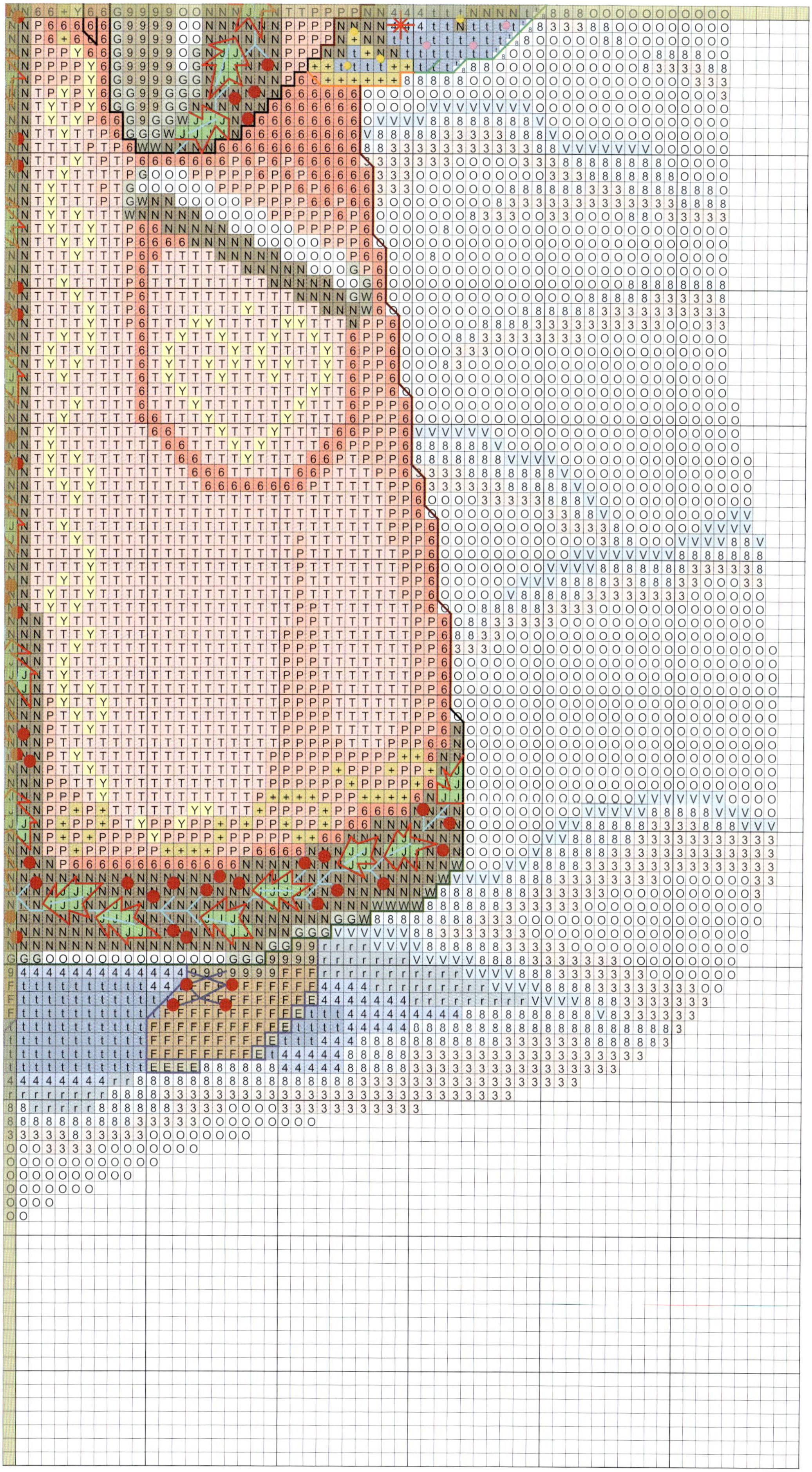

Gold area indicates last row of previous section of design.

CROSS STITCH

ANCHOR		DMC	COLOR
333	P	900	Dark Burnt Orange
340	6	919	Red Copper
881	b	945	Tawny
246	A	986	Very Dark Forest Green
244	J	987	Dark Forest Green
242	M	989	Forest Green
1040	W	3023	Light Brown Gray
397	G	3024	Very Light Brown Gray
360	N	3031	Very Dark Mocha Brown
871	<	3041	Medium Antique Violet
869	n	3743	Very Light Antique Violet
120	8	3747	Very Light Blue Violet
336	k	3771	Ultra Very Light Terra Cotta
306	+	3820	Dark Straw
002	O	3865	Winter White

HALF STITCH

(symbols appear as full stitches in chart)

ANCHOR		DMC	COLOR
300	B	745	Light Pale Yellow
023	=	818	Baby Pink
006	e	967	Very Light Apricot

FRENCH KNOT

ANCHOR		DMC	COLOR
226	•	702	Kelly Green
256	•	704	Bright Chartreuse
305	•	728	Topaz
360	•	3031	Very Dark Mocha Brown
306	•	3820	Dark Straw

BACKSTITCH

ANCHOR	DMC	COLOR
009	352	Light Coral
334	606	Bright Orange Red
256	704	Bright Chartreuse
305	728	Topaz
162	825	Dark Blue
360	839	Dark Beige Brown
379	840	Medium Beige Brown
340	919	Red Copper
246	986	Very Dark Forest Green
360	3031	Very Dark Mocha Brown
306	3820	Dark Straw
002	3865	Winter White

STAR EYELET

ANCHOR		DMC	COLOR
305	✳	728	Topaz

BEAD

MILL HILL GLASS SEED		COLOR
00557	•	Old Gold
02034	•	Autumn Flame

Nordic Santa Alphabet

CROSS STITCH

ANCHOR		DMC	COLOR
334	T	606	Bright Orange Red
256	U	704	Bright Chartreuse

Gold area indicates last row of previous section of design.

CHRISTOPHER

Nutcracker Stocking

Designed by Linda Bird

This trio of nutcrackers will watch over you and yours throughout the winter months. Stitched in a variety of colors, the stunning design brightens any seasonal display.

Notes: Please read all instructions on page 33 before beginning. Use the alphabet on pages 22-23 to chart and center the desired name on the cuff area.

Stitch Count = 152w × 247h

FABRIC

- One 18" × 26" (45.7cm × 66.0cm) piece of 14-ct. Opalescent White Metallic Aida cloth by Zweigart®

DESIGN SIZE

- 14-ct. = $10\frac{7}{8}$" × $17\frac{5}{8}$" (27.6cm × 44.8cm)

FINISHING MATERIALS

- One 20" × 14" piece of coordinating fabric for backing
- Two 20" × 14" pieces of coordinating fabric for lining
- Twisted metallic cording trim

GENERAL INSTRUCTIONS

Center the design and begin stitching. Work stem stitches with three strands of cotton embroidery floss or DMC® Light Effects floss. Work cross stitches and Algerian stars with two strands of cotton embroidery floss or DMC Light Effects floss. Use one strand of cotton embroidery floss to work backstitches. Use the accompanying alphabet chart to personalize the stocking. *Note:* Do not stitch the red outline, as it is a finishing guide. Use a pressing cloth to carefully iron the needlework from the back before finishing.

FINISHING INSTRUCTIONS

Use a $\frac{1}{2}$" seam allowance for all sewing unless otherwise specified. Center and trim the needlework to within 1" of the stitching, referring to the finishing guideline as necessary. With the wrong side up, use this as a template to cut two pieces from the right side of coordinating fabric. Flip the needlework right side up and use it as a template to cut one piece from the right side of coordinating fabric.

With right sides together, sew the stocking front to the back, sewing tight to the cording but leaving the top open. Trim the side and bottom seam allowances to $\frac{1}{4}$". Turn the stocking right side out and iron using a pressing cloth.

Sew the lining pieces together in the same manner as the stocking, but use a 1" seam allowance and leave a 4" opening along the bottom of the "foot" for turning. Trim the side and bottom seam allowances to $\frac{1}{4}$".

Leave the lining wrong side out and insert the stocking into the lining, aligning the top edges. Sew all the way around the top, sewing through all layers. Pull the stocking through the opening in the lining. Slipstitch the opening in the lining, tuck the lining inside the stocking, and press.

Hand-sew the cording around the edge of the stocking, tucking cut edges into the top of the stocking at the beginning and end. Cut a 3" × 6" strip of coordinating fabric for a hanging loop. With right sides together, fold in half lengthwise and press. Sew along the cut edge, turn, and fold in half to form a loop. Attach to the top left inner corner of the stocking with a few hand-stitches.

Chart Layout

A	B
C	D
E	F

Nutcracker Stocking B

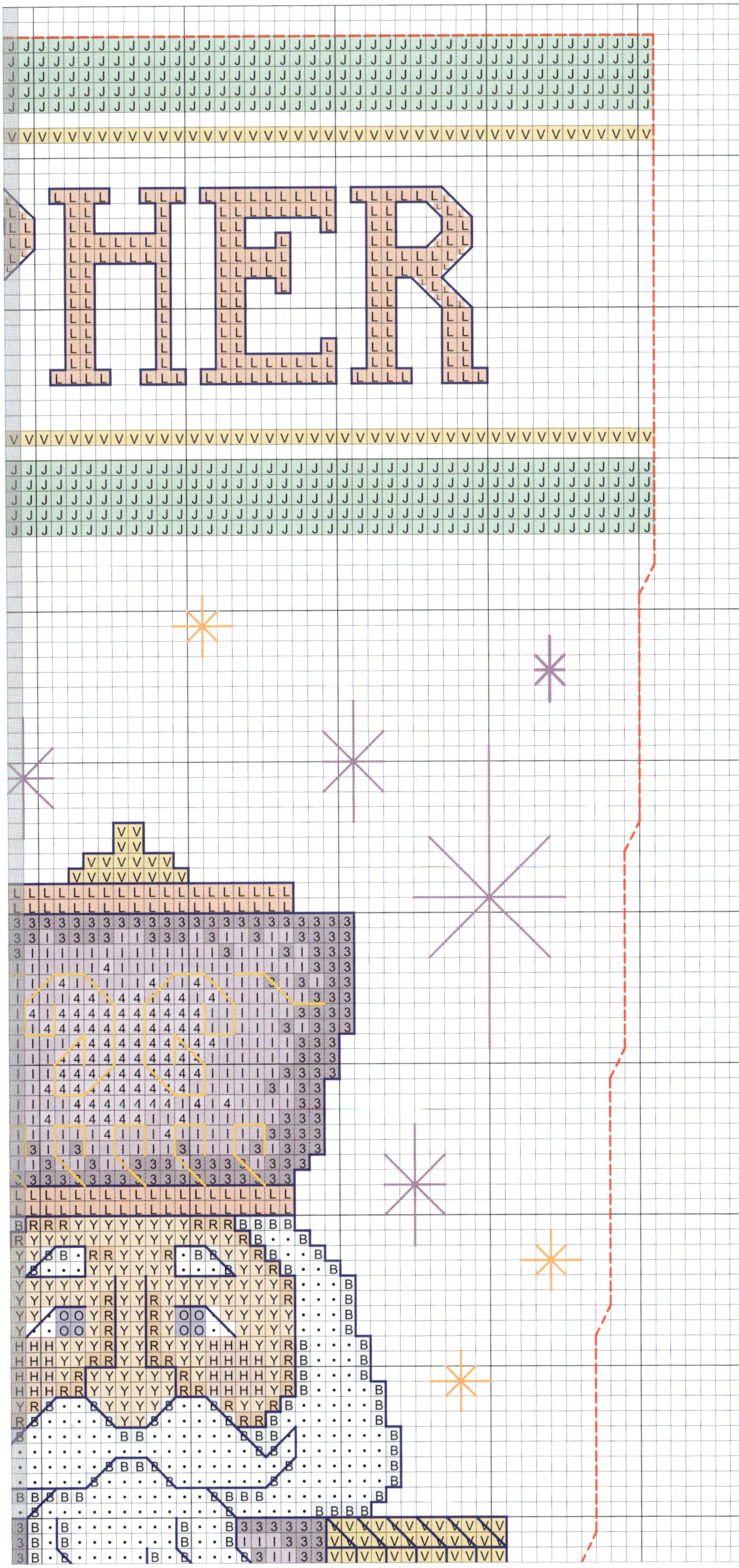

CROSS STITCH

ANCHOR		DMC	COLOR
002	•	White	White
403	X	310	Black
979	O	312	Very Dark Baby Blue
9046	K	321	Christmas Red
978	N	322	Dark Baby Blue
977	E	334	Medium Baby Blue
310	M	434	Light Brown
1046	S	435	Very Light Brown
1045	P	436	Tan
102	3	550	Very Dark Violet
099	I	552	Medium Violet
098	4	553	Violet
046	L	666	Bright Christmas Red
923	J	699	Christmas Green
228	F	700	Bright Christmas Green
305	U	725	Topaz
361	2	738	Very Light Tan
1012	Y	754	Light Peach
234	B	762	Very Light Pearl Gray
336	R	3771	Ultra Very Light Terra Cotta
1013	H	3778	Light Terra Cotta
236	A	3799	Very Dark Pewter Gray
035	8	3801	Light Christmas Red
306	7	3852	Very Dark Straw

	DMC LIGHT EFFECTS	COLOR
V	E3821	Light Gold
6	E168	Silver

BACKSTITCH

ANCHOR	DMC	COLOR
403	310	Black

STEM STITCH

ANCHOR	DMC	COLOR
978	322	Dark Baby Blue
046	666	Bright Christmas Red

DMC LIGHT EFFECTS	COLOR
E3821	Light Gold

ALGERIAN STAR

DMC LIGHT EFFECTS	COLOR
E3821	Light Gold

ALGERIAN STAR EYELET

DMC LIGHT EFFECTS	COLOR
E3821	Light Gold

Finishing Guideline (do not stitch)

Gray area indicates last row of previous section of design.

Nutcracker Stocking C

Gray area indicates last row of previous section of design.

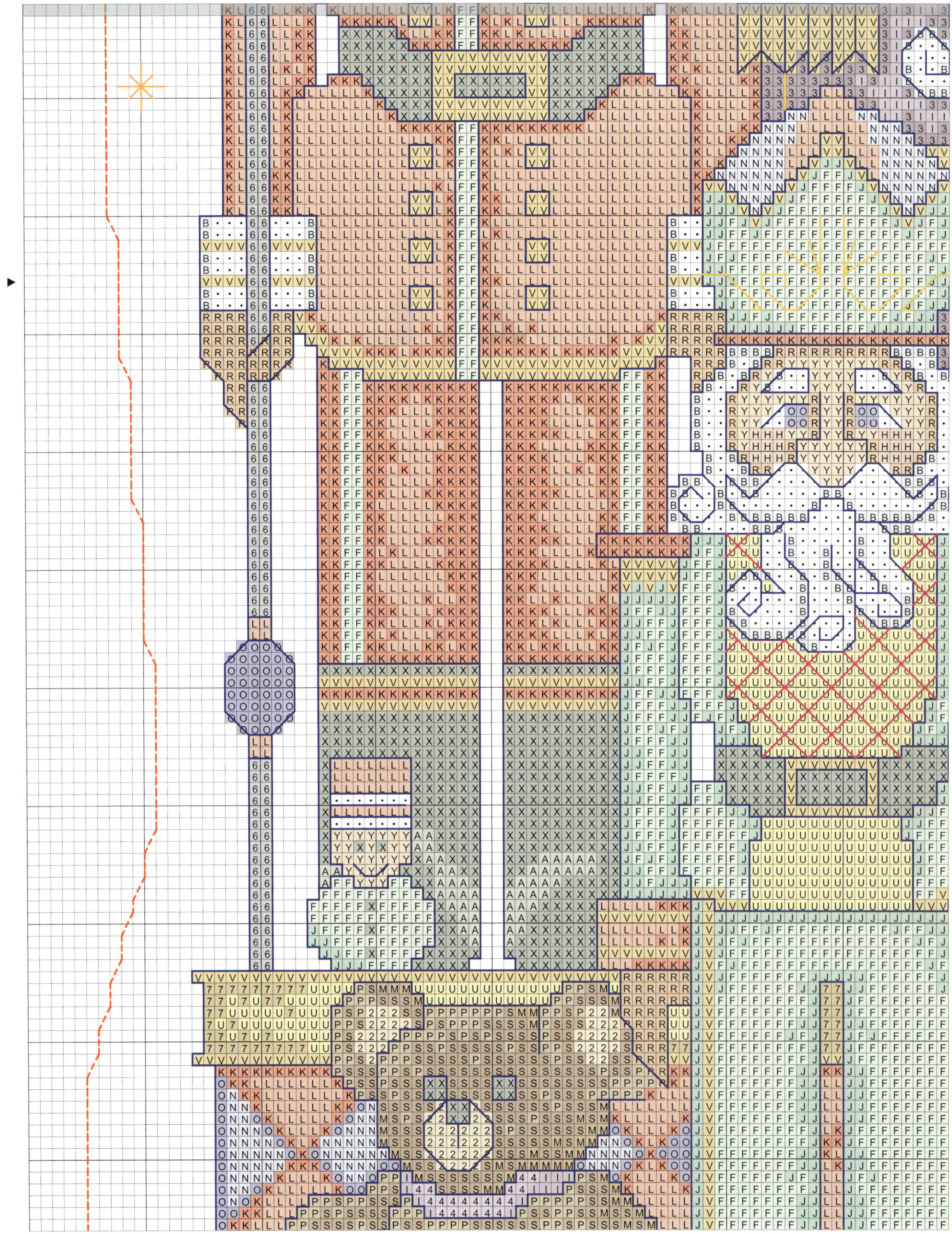

Note: Color key can be found on pages 19 and 23.

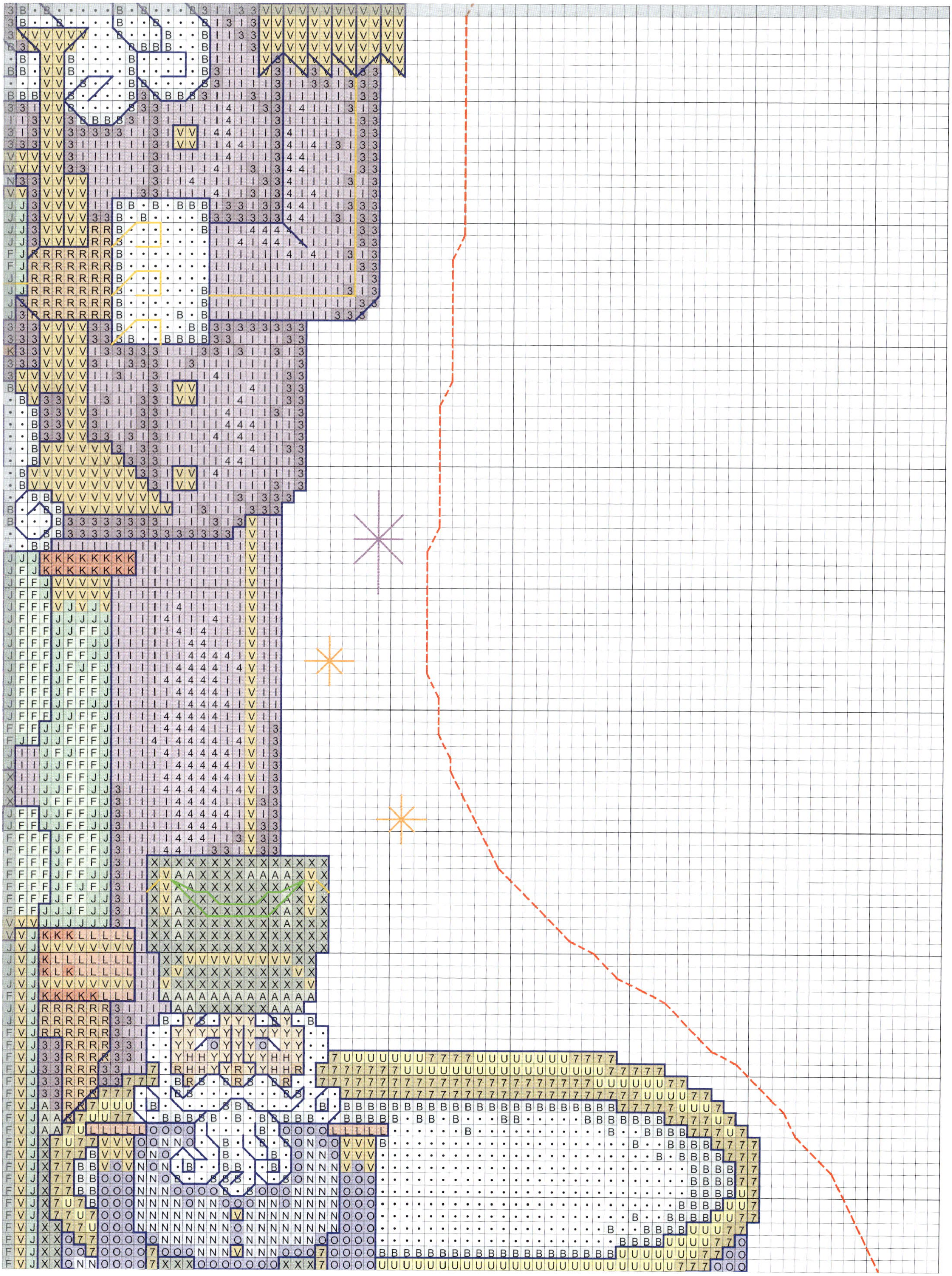

Gray area indicates last row of previous section of design.

Nutcracker Stocking E

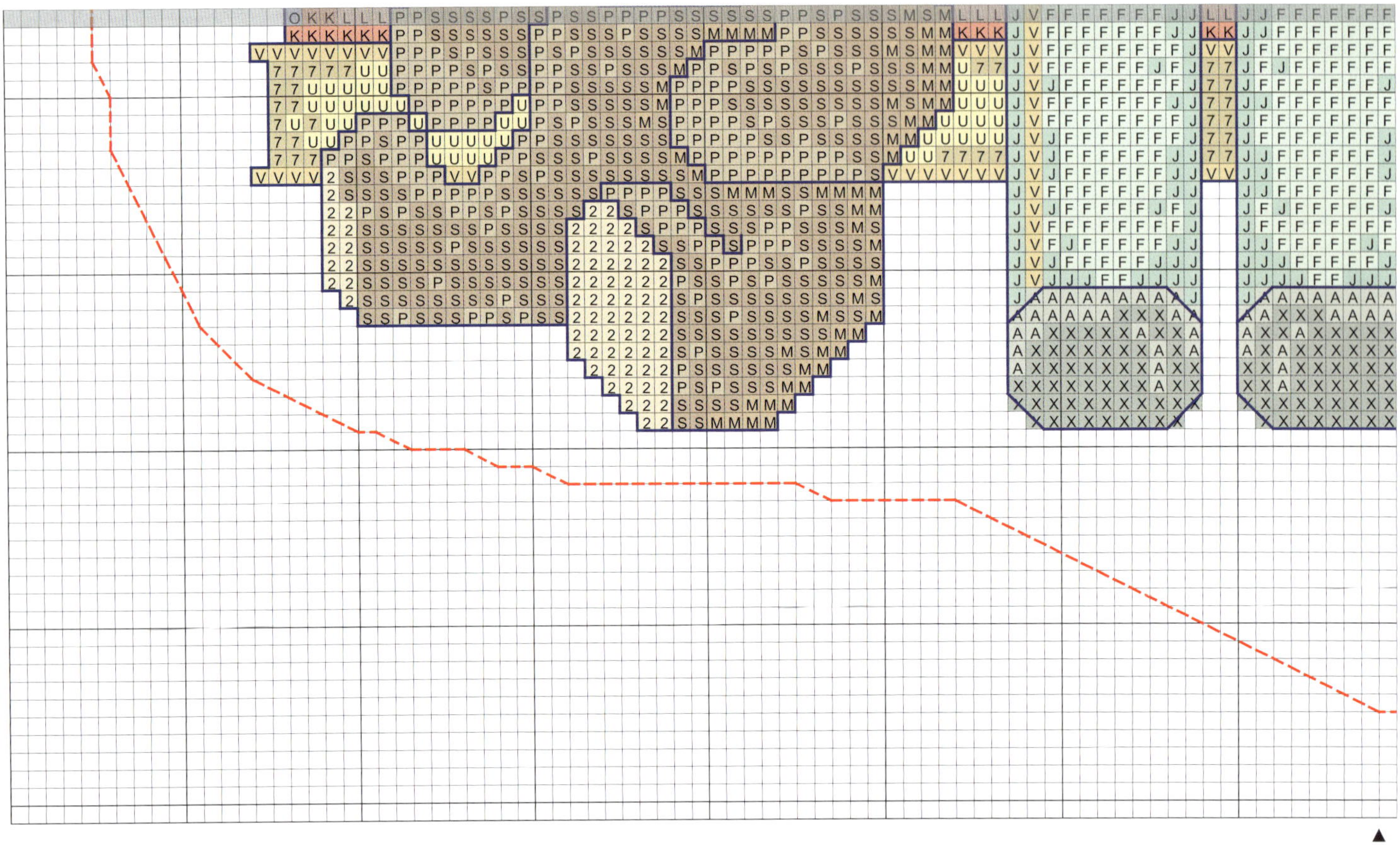

Nutcracker Alphabet

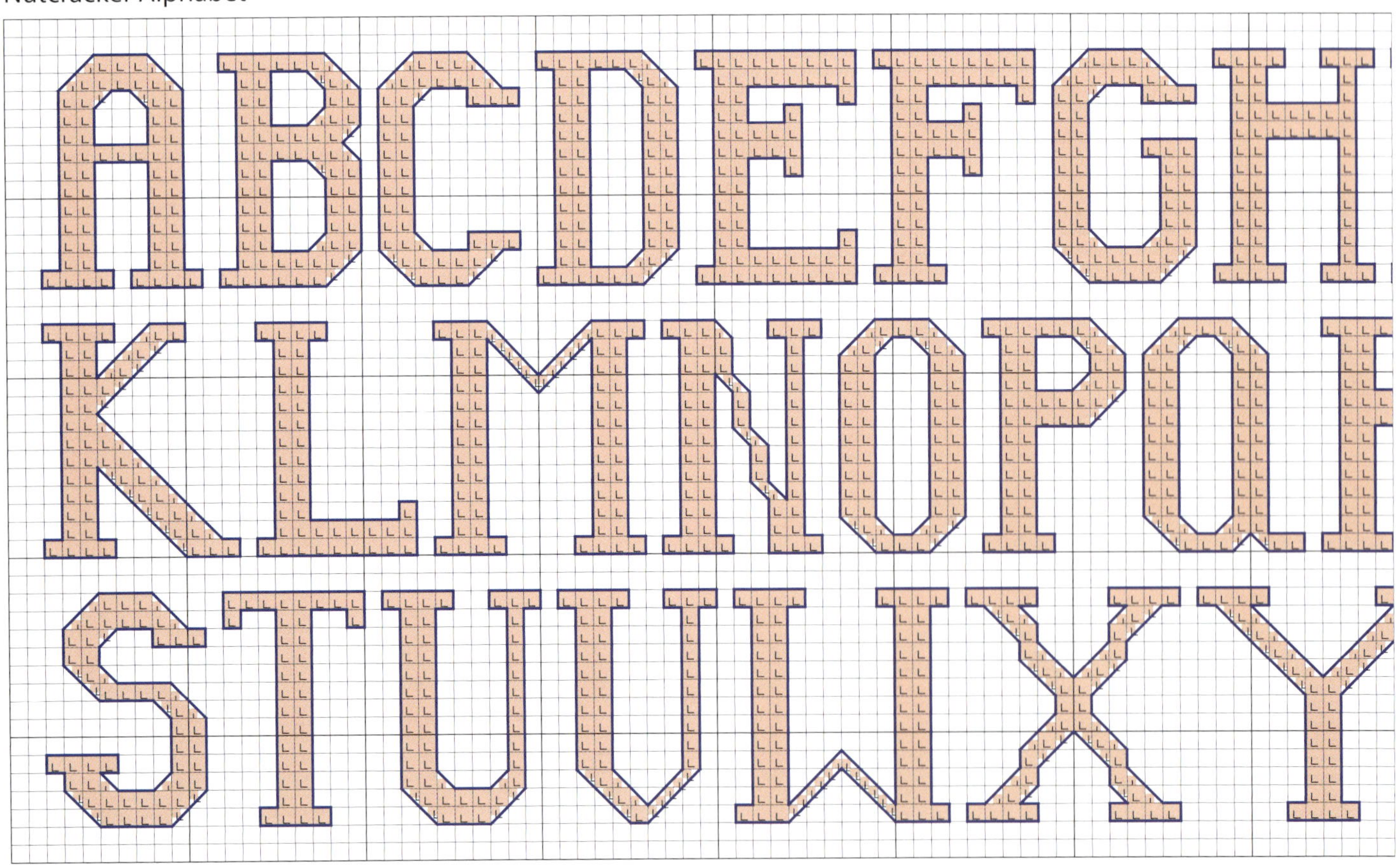

Nutcracker Stocking F

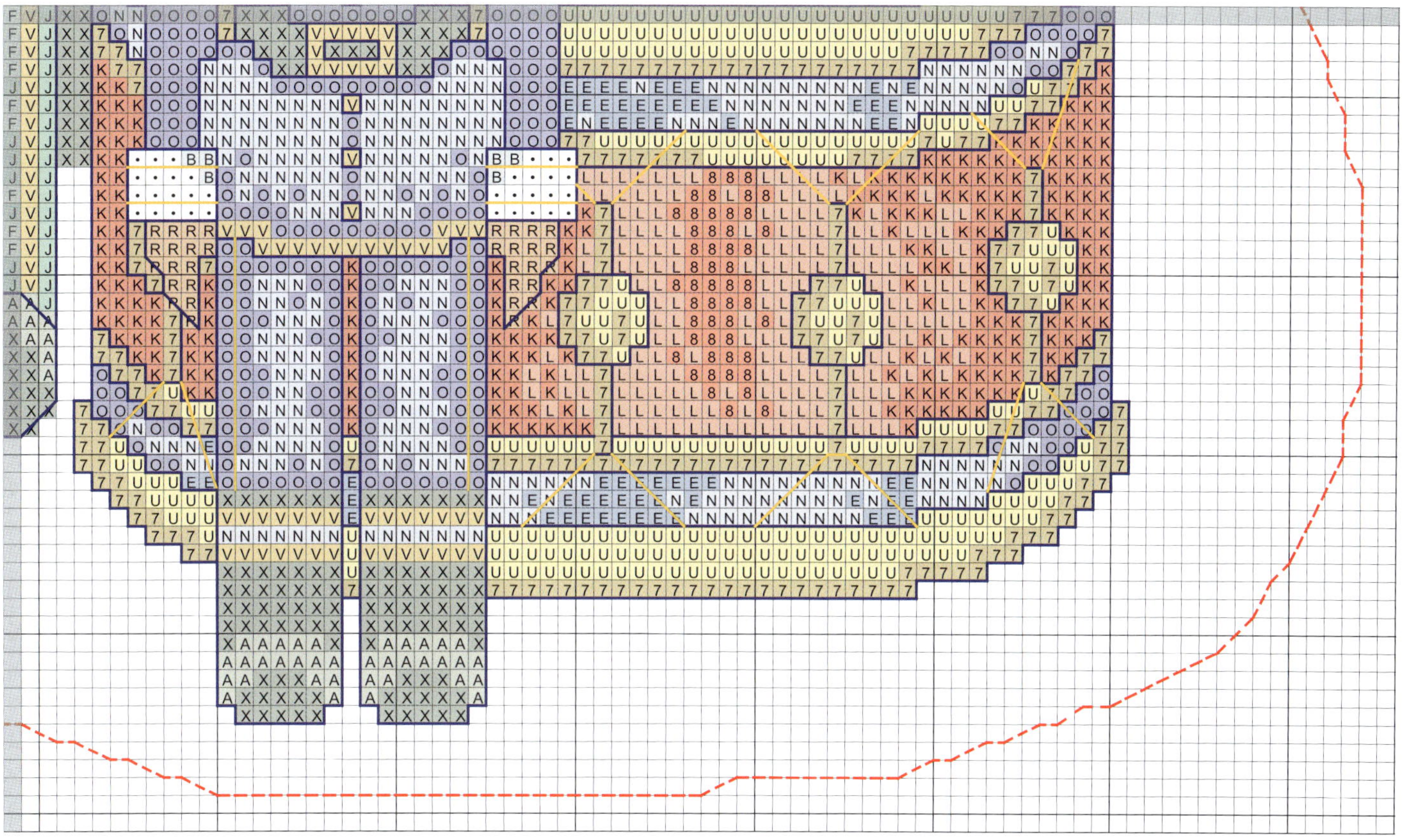

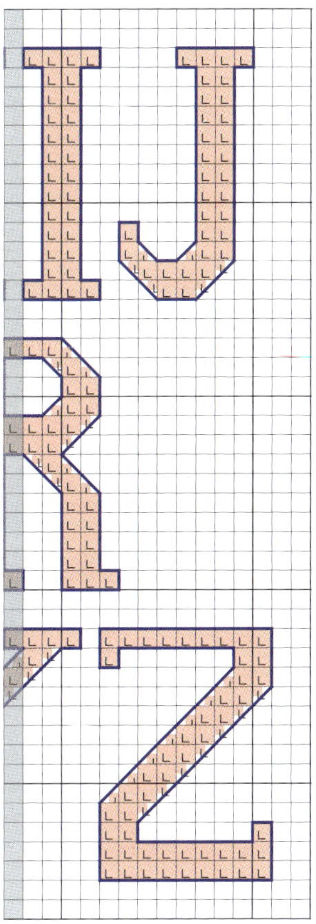

CROSS STITCH

ANCHOR		DMC	COLOR
002	•	White	White
403	X	310	Black
979	O	312	Very Dark Baby Blue
9046	K	321	Christmas Red
978	N	322	Dark Baby Blue
977	E	334	Medium Baby Blue
310	M	434	Light Brown
1046	S	435	Very Light Brown
1045	P	436	Tan
102	3	550	Very Dark Violet
099	I	552	Medium Violet
098	4	553	Violet
046	L	666	Bright Christmas Red
923	J	699	Christmas Green
228	F	700	Bright Christmas Green
305	U	725	Topaz
361	2	738	Very Light Tan
1012	Y	754	Light Peach
234	B	762	Very Light Pearl Gray
336	R	3771	Ultra Very Light Terra Cotta
1013	H	3778	Light Terra Cotta
236	A	3799	Very Dark Pewter Gray
035	8	3801	Light Christmas Red
306	7	3852	Very Dark Straw

	DMC LIGHT EFFECTS	COLOR
V	E3821	Light Gold
6	E168	Silver

BACKSTITCH

ANCHOR	DMC	COLOR
403	310	Black

STEM STITCH

ANCHOR	DMC	COLOR
978	322	Dark Baby Blue
046	666	Bright Christmas Red

DMC LIGHT EFFECTS	COLOR
E3821	Light Gold

ALGERIAN STAR

DMC LIGHT EFFECTS	COLOR
E3821	Light Gold

ALGERIAN STAR EYELET

DMC LIGHT EFFECTS	COLOR
E3821	Light Gold

Finishing Guideline (do not stitch)

Gray area indicates last row of previous section of design.

Jolly Snowman Stocking

This cheerful stocking features a playful snowman and is sure to be a favorite with both young and old. Use the accompanying alphabet to personalize it for a loved one!

Designed by Alma Lynne Hayden

Notes: Please read all instructions on page 33 before beginning. Use the alphabet on pages 25-27 to chart and center the desired name on the cuff area.

Stitch Count = 134w × 212h

FABRIC

• One 18" × 23" (45.7cm × 58.4cm) piece of 28-ct. White Jobelan® by Wichelt Imports (stitched over two threads)

DESIGN SIZE

• 28-ct. = 9⅝" × 15⅛" (24.4cm × 38.4cm)

FINISHING MATERIALS

• 1 yard of coordinating fabric for lining and back
• ½ yard of lightweight fusible interfacing
• Matching sewing thread

GENERAL INSTRUCTIONS

Center the design and begin stitching over two fabric threads (chart starts on page 28). Work cross stitches and quarter stitches with two strands of cotton embroidery floss. Use one strand of cotton embroidery floss to work backstitches and French knots. Use the accompanying alphabet chart to personalize the stocking. *Note:* Do not stitch the outline around the stocking, as it is the finishing guideline. Use a pressing cloth to carefully iron the needlework from the back before finishing.

FINISHING INSTRUCTIONS

Use a ¼" seam allowance for all sewing unless otherwise specified. Center lightweight fusible interfacing on the wrong side of the needlework and fuse into place following the manufacturer's instructions. Trim the needlework to within ¼" of the stitching on the sides and bottom and to within ¾" of the stitching on the top, referring to the finishing guideline as necessary.

With the wrong side up, use the needlework as a template to cut two pieces from the right side of coordinating fabric. Flip the needlework right side up and use it as a template to cut one piece from the right side of coordinating fabric.

With wrong sides together, topstitch the stocking front to the back, leaving the top open. Turn wrong side out. With right sides together, sew the lining pieces together along the sides and bottom, leaving the top open and a 4" opening along the bottom of the "foot" for turning.

Leave the lining wrong side out and insert the stocking into the lining, aligning the top edges. Sew all the way around the top and pull the stocking through the opening in the lining. Slipstitch the opening in the lining, tuck the lining inside the stocking, and press.

Cut a 1½" × 8½" strip of coordinating fabric. Fold in half lengthwise with wrong sides together and press to create a binding. With right sides together, sew to the top front edge of the stocking. Press the binding to the inside of the stocking and hand-sew in place.

Cut 1½"-wide bias strips of coordinating fabric and piece together to form one 42"-long strip. Fold in half lengthwise with wrong sides together and press to create a binding. With right sides together and the cut edges aligned, begin at the top left corner of the stocking, folding the short end of the binding ¼" to the wrong side and tacking in place. Sew the binding around the needlework, following along the edge of the stitching. Turn the excess binding to the back to create a hanging loop on the top right corner of the stocking. Press the binding to the back and hand-sew in place. Fold the hanging loop to the back and attach with a few hand-stitches.

Stocking Chart Layout

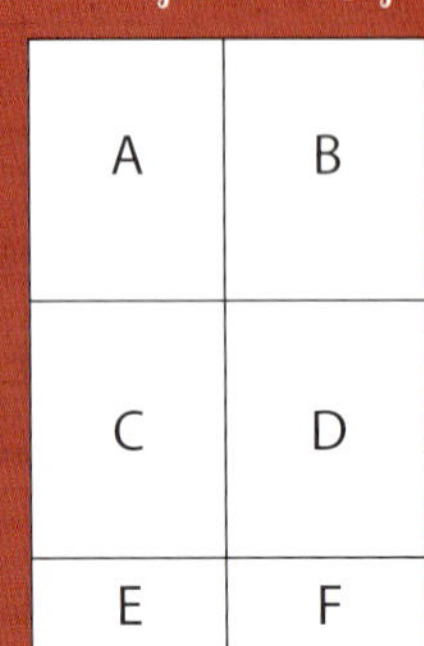

Jolly Snowman Alphabet A

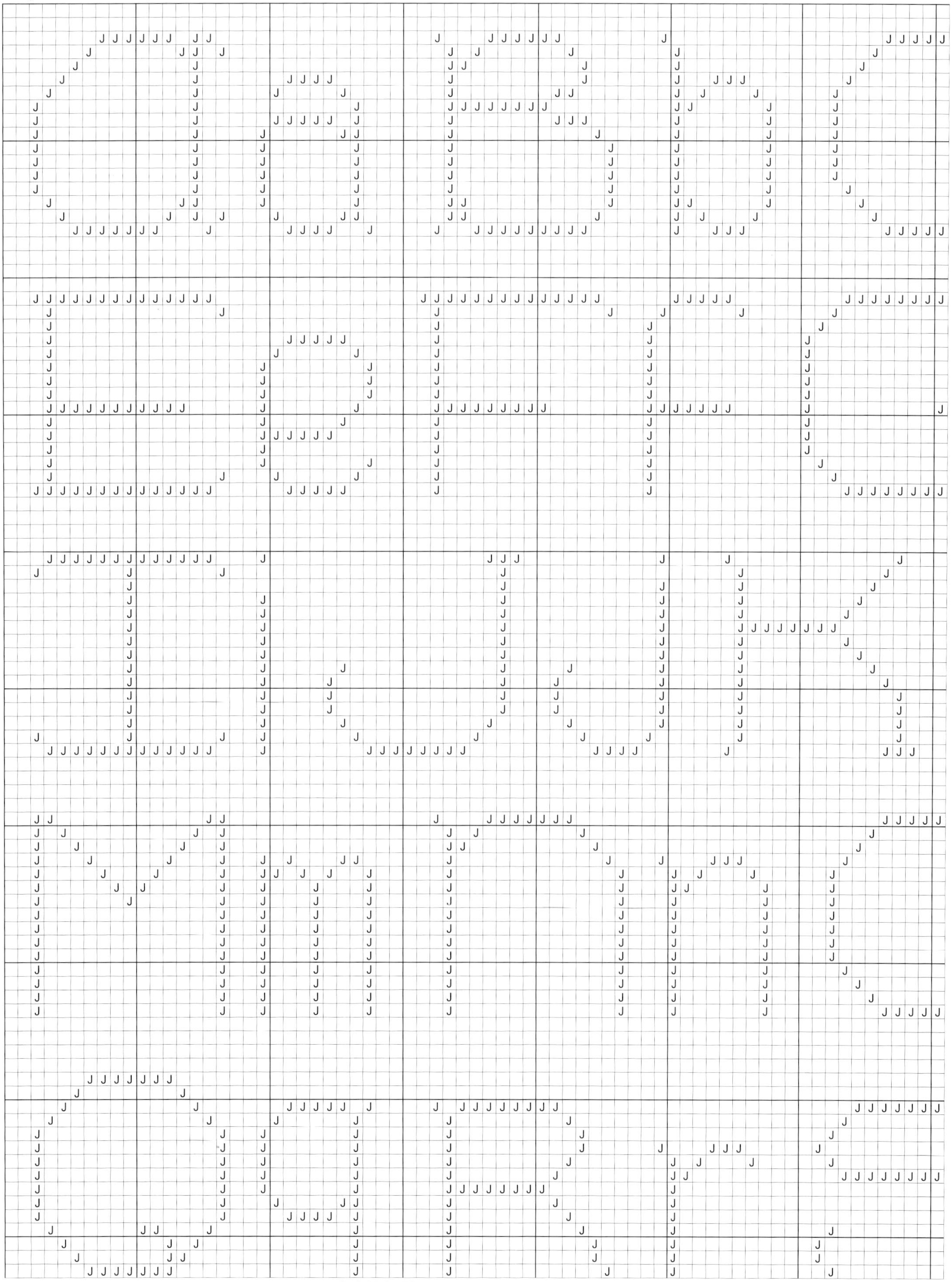

CROSS STITCH

ANCHOR		DMC	COLOR
255	J	907	Light Parrot Green

Jolly Snowman Alphabet B

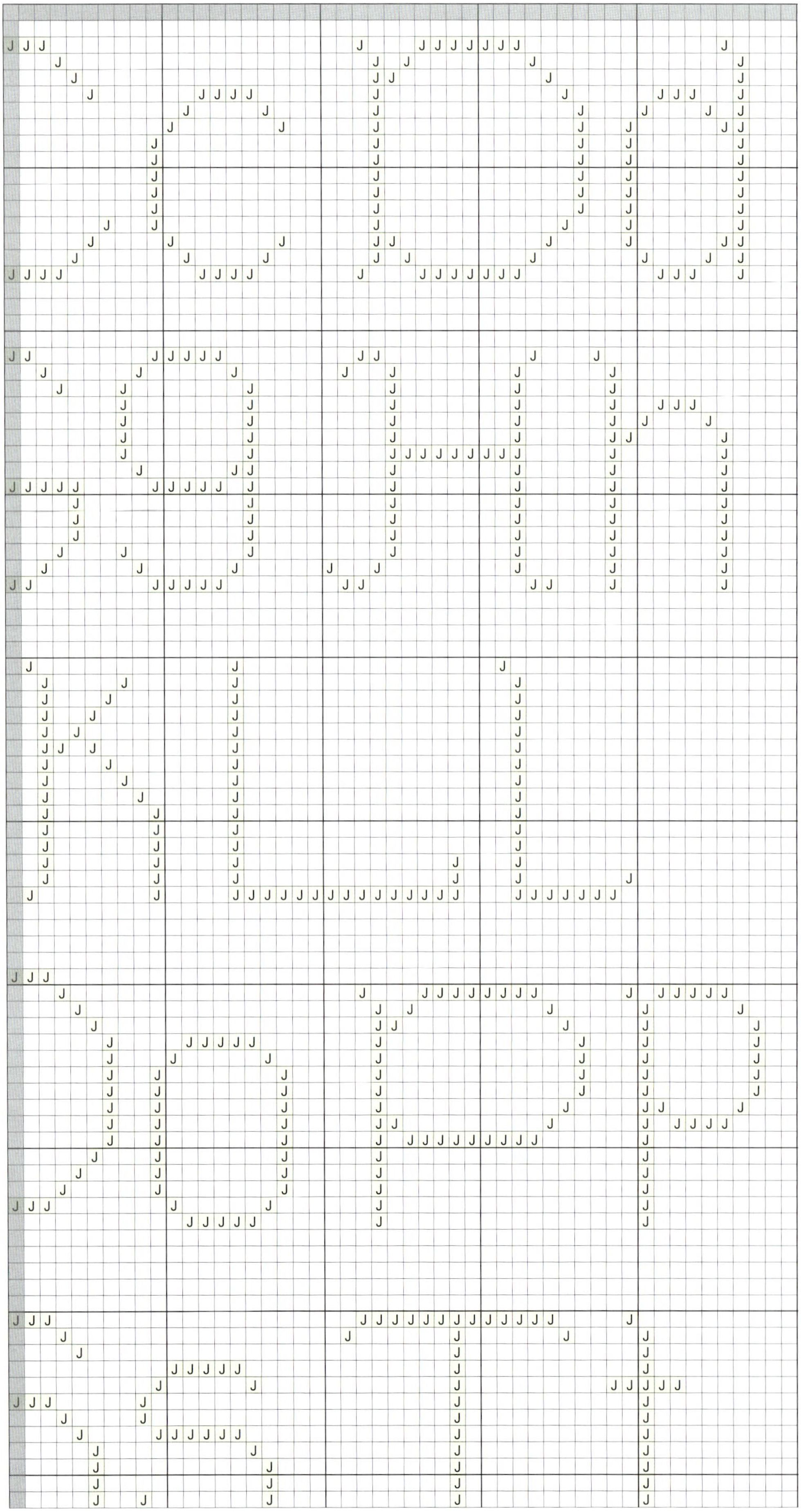

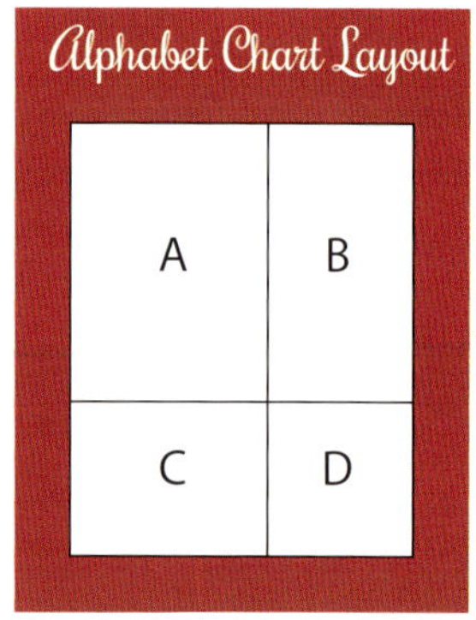

CROSS STITCH

ANCHOR		DMC	COLOR
255	J	907	Light Parrot Green

Gray area indicates last row of previous section of design.

Jolly Snowman Alphabet C

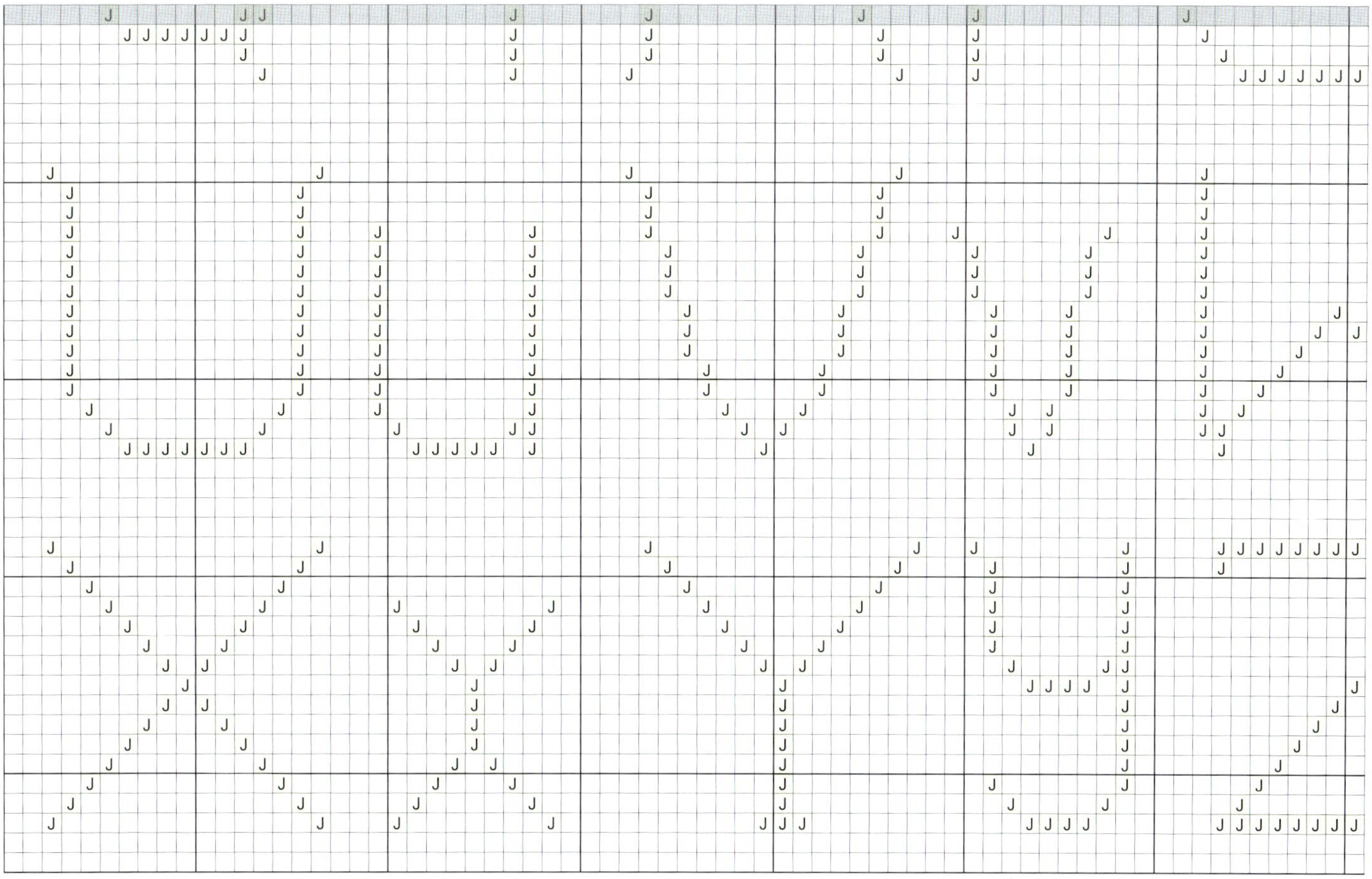

Jolly Snowman Alphabet D

CROSS STITCH

ANCHOR		DMC	COLOR
255	J	907	Light Parrot Green

Gray area indicates last row of previous section of design.

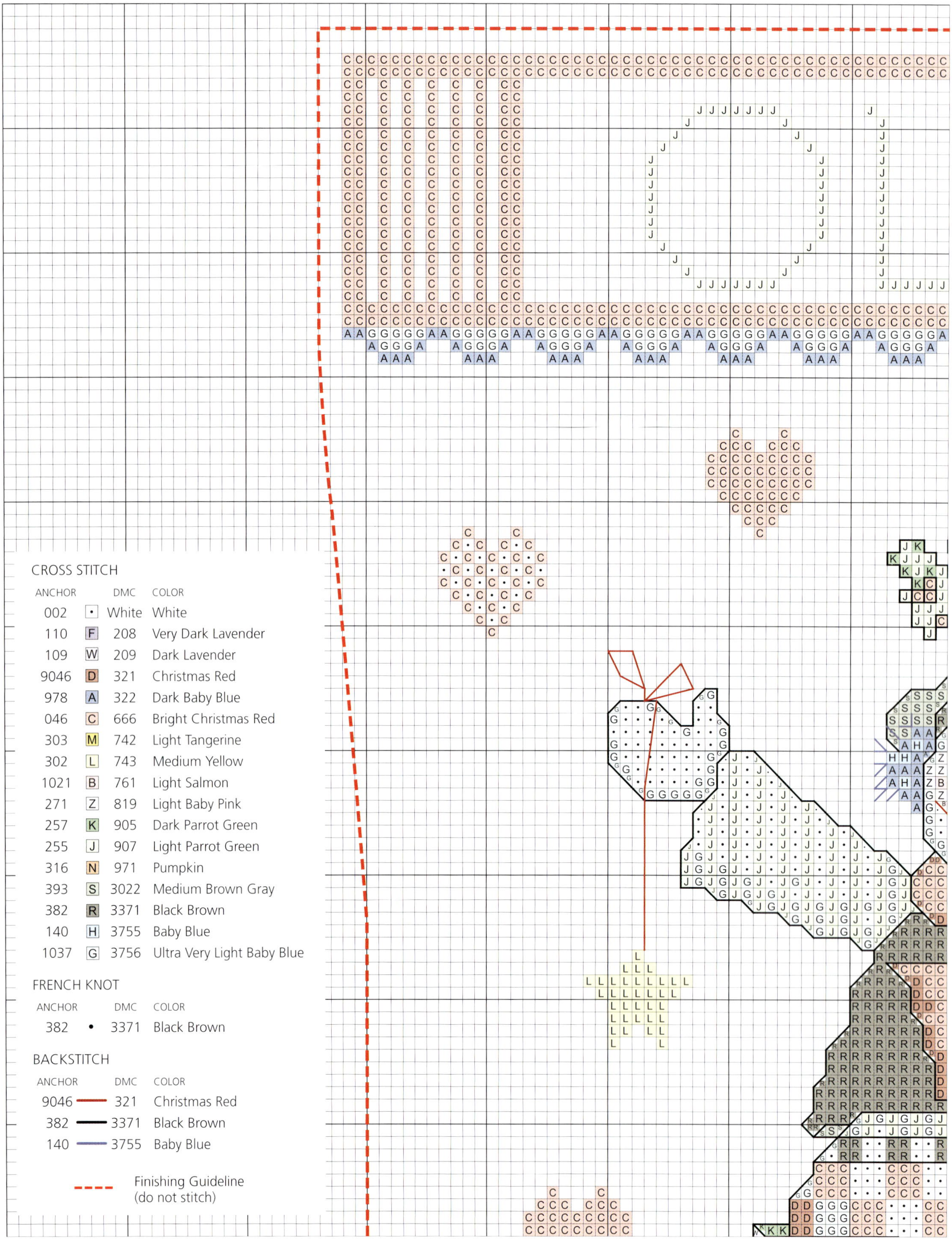

CROSS STITCH

ANCHOR		DMC	COLOR
002	•	White	White
110	F	208	Very Dark Lavender
109	W	209	Dark Lavender
9046	D	321	Christmas Red
978	A	322	Dark Baby Blue
046	C	666	Bright Christmas Red
303	M	742	Light Tangerine
302	L	743	Medium Yellow
1021	B	761	Light Salmon
271	Z	819	Light Baby Pink
257	K	905	Dark Parrot Green
255	J	907	Light Parrot Green
316	N	971	Pumpkin
393	S	3022	Medium Brown Gray
382	R	3371	Black Brown
140	H	3755	Baby Blue
1037	G	3756	Ultra Very Light Baby Blue

FRENCH KNOT

ANCHOR		DMC	COLOR
382	•	3371	Black Brown

BACKSTITCH

ANCHOR	DMC	COLOR
9046	321	Christmas Red
382	3371	Black Brown
140	3755	Baby Blue

Finishing Guideline (do not stitch)

Gray area indicates last row of previous section of design.

Jolly Snowman Stocking B

Jolly Snowman Stocking C

Gray area indicates last row of previous section of design.

Jolly Snowman Stocking D

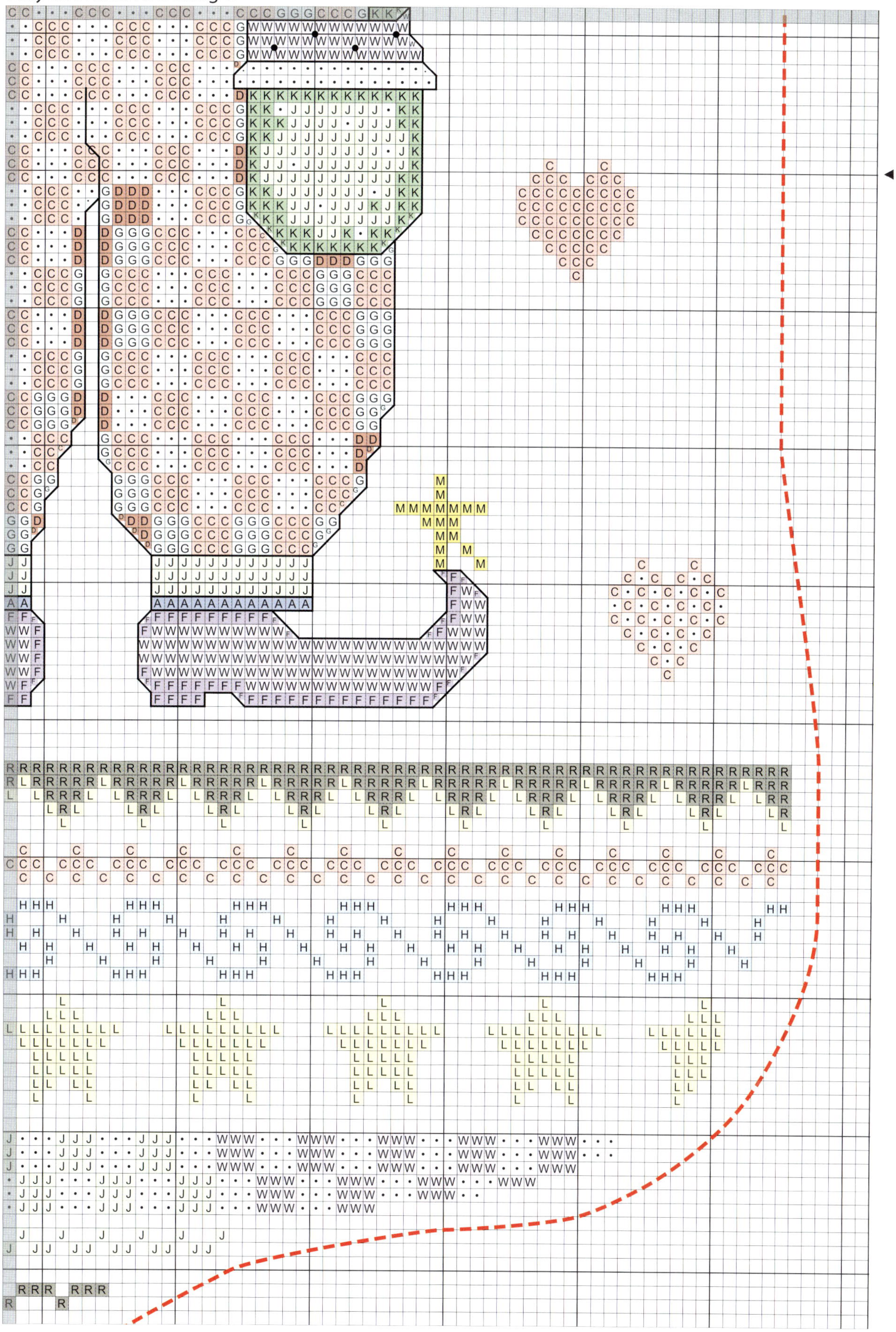

Note: Color key can be found on pages 28 and 32.

Jolly Snowman Stocking E

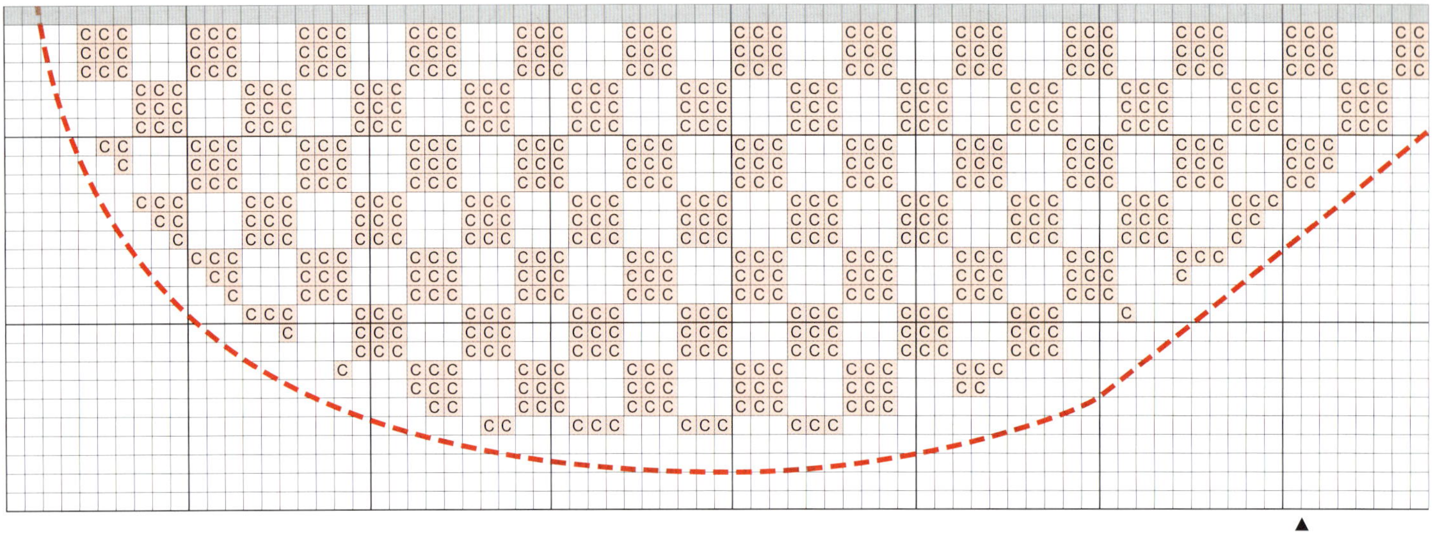

Jolly Snowman Stocking F

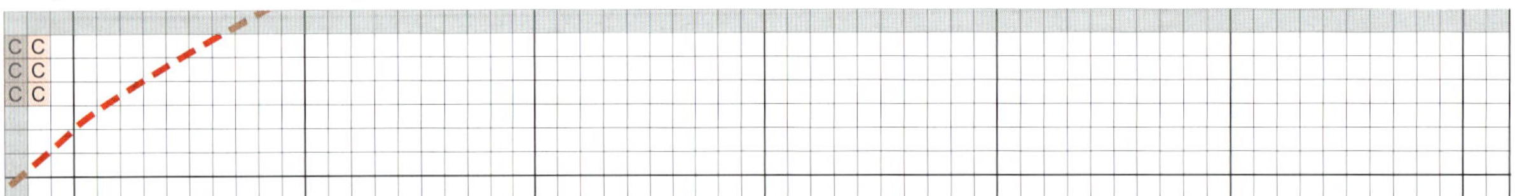

CROSS STITCH

ANCHOR		DMC	COLOR
002	•	White	White
110	F	208	Very Dark Lavender
109	W	209	Dark Lavender
9046	D	321	Christmas Red
978	A	322	Dark Baby Blue
046	C	666	Bright Christmas Red
303	M	742	Light Tangerine
302	L	743	Medium Yellow
1021	B	761	Light Salmon
271	Z	819	Light Baby Pink
257	K	905	Dark Parrot Green
255	J	907	Light Parrot Green
316	N	971	Pumpkin
393	S	3022	Medium Brown Gray

CROSS STITCH

ANCHOR		DMC	COLOR
140	H	3755	Baby Blue
1037	G	3756	Ultra Very Light Baby Blue

FRENCH KNOT

ANCHOR		DMC	COLOR
382	•	3371	Black Brown

BACKSTITCH

ANCHOR		DMC	COLOR
9046	—	321	Christmas Red
382	—	3371	Black Brown
140	—	3755	Baby Blue

- - - - Finishing Guideline (do not stitch)

Gray area indicates last row of previous section of design.

Project Tip

Storing Seasonal Needlework

To ensure that seasonal needlework items stay looking their best from year to year, it is important to store them properly. Washable items should be cleaned with a mild soap and water solution to remove any stains or dirt. Allow pieces to dry completely so no moisture remains. Wrap all items in acid-free tissue paper and place in an acid-free box for storage. (Plastic bags or bins can trap moisture and cause mildew and staining.) The box should then be stored in a dark place, free from humidity and extreme temperatures; an interior closet is best. Linens should be refolded twice a year to prevent any fabric creases from becoming permanent.